The Plate Escape

FLAVOR BURSTING VEGAN AND VEGETARIAN RECIPES BY
KELLY FROM @POSITRAVELTY

KELLY CASTILLE WORKMAN

About the Author:

Kelly and her husband, Kody, owners of @positravelty on Instagram, have traveled the world for years, chasing the most beautiful destinations on the planet. Aside from their photography and videography passions they are also very much inspired by food and the culture behind it. Even before their travels cooking was a constant in Kelly's life. Having been very active in the fitness world, participating in and winning physique competitions, eating healthy was a must, but it needed to be done with no compromise to flavor. The recipes in this book have been masterfully curated by Kelly to be healthier and so delicious that the urge to go in for seconds can be done guilt free.

CONTENTS

MAINS

Breakfast

Apple Cinnamon Oatmeal Cups

(Substitute Flax Eggs to make vegan)

Recipe makes 12 muffins

- 1 granny smith apple, peeled, cored and diced
- 3 cups old fashioned oats
- 1/3 cup pure maple syrup
- 1 teaspoon baking powder
- 1 scoop vanilla (or unflavored) protein powder
- 1 cup unsweetened almond milk
- 2 large eggs
- 1 teaspoon vanilla extract
- 1.5 teaspoons cinnamon
- Pinch of salt

1. Preheat the oven to 350 degrees F.
2. In a large mixing bowl, combine the oats, cinnamon, baking powder, protein powder, and salt and stir to combine.
3. In a separate bowl, whisk together the eggs, milk, maple syrup and vanilla extract until smooth. Add the wet ingredients to the dry ingredients and mix well. Add the chopped apples and stir.
4. Line a standard 12 count muffin pan with cupcake liners and evenly pour the mixture.
5. Bake for 25-30 minutes, or until the tops are lightly brown and firm.
6. Let cool before peeling off the cupcake liners and enjoy!

Loaded Avocado Toast

Recipe makes 2 servings

- 2 thick slices of sourdough bread
- 2 eggs (one egg per toast)
- 2 small avocados or 1 large avocado
- Handful of cherry tomatoes, halved
- 1/2 cup frozen peas
- 1 lime
- Handful fresh spinach or arugula
- Crumbled feta cheese, to top
- 1 teaspoon salt
- 1 teaspoon black pepper
- 1 teaspoon Everything But The Bagel Seasoning
- Pinch of red pepper flakes (optional, for heat)

Optional topping:

- 4 oz smoked salmon (for a non-vegetarian option)

1. Start by making the seasoned mashed avocado. Smash the avocado with a fork in a bowl and add the juice of 1 lime, salt, black pepper and red pepper flakes. Set aside.

2. For the eggs: you can choose how you want to cook them! Eggs are delicious with the recipe any way you'd like! Poached, fried, scrambled, sunny side up...you choose! Here is when you cook your eggs.

3. While the eggs cook, heat a small amount of olive oil in a nonstick pan over low-medium heat then add the peas and spinach or arugula and cook until the peas are hot and the greens are wilted.

4. Toast the sourdough bread and assemble by adding guacamole to the toast, then a slice of smoked salmon (optional), then the peas and spinach/arugula, and top with the eggs. Crumble the feta cheese on top and sprinkle with Everything But The Bagel Seasoning. Plate with the halved cherry tomatoes and enjoy!

Almond Flour Banana Bread

(Vegetarian; Vegan if eggs are substituted for flax eggs)

- 3 ripe bananas
- 2 eggs
- 2.5 cups almond flour
- 1 teaspoon vanilla extract
- 1/4 cup pure maple syrup
- 1/4 cup coconut oil, melted
- 1 teaspoon cinnamon
- 1 teaspoon baking powder
- 1 teaspoon baking soda
- Pinch of salt

Optional add-ins:

- Chopped walnuts or pecans
- Chocolate chips
- Raisins

1. Preheat oven to 350 degrees F.
2. Spray a 9x5 loaf pan with nonstick spray and set aside.
3. In a large mixing bowl, mash the bananas with a fork. Add the eggs, maple syrup, coconut oil and vanilla extract and mix well.
4. Stir in the cinnamon, almond flour, salt, baking soda and baking powder, along with any add-ins of your choice and mix well.
5. Pour the mixture into the loaf pan and bake for 45 minutes, or until a toothpick comes out clean when inserted into the center.
6. Allow to cool after baking before slicing.

Spinach Banana Protein Oat Muffins

(Vegetarian; Substitute Flax Eggs to make vegan)

Recipe makes 12 muffins

- 3 handfuls fresh spinach
- 2 ripe bananas
- 2 eggs
- 1/3 cup unsweetened almond or oat milk
- 1/4 cup pure maple syrup
- 1 cup almond flour
- 1 cup oat flour (pulse old fashioned oats in a blender until a flour like consistency forms)
- 1 teaspoon baking powder
- 1 teaspoon baking soda
- 1 teaspoon cinnamon
- 1 teaspoon vanilla extract
- 1 scoop vanilla protein powder
- 1/4 cup flaxseed meal
- 1/4 cup coconut oil, melted
- Pinch of salt

1. Preheat oven to 375 degrees F. Line a muffin tin with 12 liners and set aside.
2. Add the bananas, eggs, milk, maple syrup, spinach and vanilla extract in a blender and blend until smooth.
3. Pour the batter into a large mixing bowl, then add the coconut oil, cinnamon, salt, baking powder, baking soda, vanilla protein powder, oat flour and almond flour and whisk until smooth.
4. Evenly pour the batter into the lined muffin tin and bake for 25 minutes, or until a toothpick comes out clean when inserted into the center.

Blueberry Banana Oat Muffins

(Substitute Flax Eggs to make vegan)

Recipe makes 12 muffins

- 2 very ripe bananas
- 1 cup blueberries
- 2 cups old fashioned oats
- 2 eggs
- 1 teaspoon baking powder
- 1 teaspoon vanilla extract
- 2 tablespoons chia seeds
- 1/3 cup pure maple syrup
- 1 scoop vegan vanilla protein powder

1. Preheat the oven to 425 degrees F.
2. Line a muffin tin with 12 cupcake liners and set aside.
3. In a mixing bowl, mash the bananas with a fork.
4. Beat the eggs and add the rest of the ingredients, except for the blueberries, to the bananas and mix well.
5. Gently stir in the blueberries.
6. Evenly spoon the batter into the muffin tin and bake for 15 minutes.

Pumpkin Pistachio Energy Bites V+

(Vegan)

- 10 pitted dates
- 1/3 pure pumpkin, canned
- 1/3 cup oats
- 1/2 scoop vegan vanilla protein powder
- 1/2 teaspoon cinnamon
- 1/2 teaspoon pumpkin pie spice
- 1/2 teaspoon vanilla extract
- Pinch of salt
- 1/2 cup raw pistachios
- 1/4 cup raw almonds

1. Add the pistachios and almonds in a blender or food processor and pulse until finely chopped or ground. Pour into a bowl and set aside.

2. Next, add all of the remaining ingredients to the same blender or food processor and blend until smooth. It shouldn't be completely smooth though, as you will want some texture.

3. Using your hands or a spoon, scoop and roll the mixture into equal bite sized balls.

4. Roll each ball in the dry nut mixture to coat and store in the refrigerator.

Berry Almond Muffins

(Vegetarian; Substitute Flax Eggs to make vegan)

Recipe makes 12 muffins

- 2 eggs
- 1/2 cup unsweetened almond milk
- 1/4 cup pure maple syrup
- 1/4 cup coconut oil, melted
- 1 teaspoon almond extract
- 1 teaspoon vanilla extract
- 2 teaspoons baking powder
- 1 teaspoon baking soda
- 1 tsp cinnamon
- Pinch of salt
- 1 cup unsweetened coconut flakes
- 1 cup almond flour
- 1 cup oat flour (pulse oats in a blender to make a "flour")
- 2 cups berries (any kind), fresh or frozen - I like to use cherries, blueberries, and raspberries
- Sliced almonds, optional for topping

1. Preheat oven to 375 degrees F and line a muffin tin with 12 liners.

2. In a large mixing bowl, add the eggs, almond milk, maple syrup, coconut oil, almond & vanilla extract, baking powder, baking soda, cinnamon and salt. Whisk well.

3. Next add in the almond flour, oat flour, and coconut flakes and stir to combine. Add 1 cup of berries and gently mix in.

4. Using a spoon, evenly divide the batter into the lined muffin tin and top with the remaining 1 cup of berries on top. Gently press the berries into the batter and top with the sliced almonds.

5. Bake for 32-35 minutes then let cool for about 10 minutes in the tin before eating.

Apricot Almond Energy Bars

- 1 cup pitted Medjool dates
- 1 cup dried apricots
- 1/2 teaspoon cinnamon
- 2 tablespoons chia seeds
- 1 cup raw almonds (walnuts or pecans can also be used)
- Optional: chocolate or white chocolate chips

1. Place the almonds in a blender or food processor, and pulse into chopped, small bits. Place in a bowl and set aside.

2. Using the same blender or food processor, add the dates, apricots, chia seeds and cinnamon and pulse until a sticky paste forms. Texture is a good thing here, but you don't want any large chunks, so you may have to scrape the sides with a spatula and blend a few times.

3. Line a 9x5 baking dish with parchment paper and add the blended dates and apricots with the crushed almonds and chocolate chips, if desired. Using your hands, mix together well and then press down into the pan.

4. Refrigerate for about 30 minutes and then cut into squares and enjoy!

Roasted Chickpea & Sweet Potato Hash V+

(Vegan)

Recipe makes approx 4 servings

- 2 sweet potatoes, peeled and chopped into cubes
- 1 onion, chopped
- 1 red bell pepper, chopped
- 1 15 oz can chickpeas, drained and rinsed
- 1 teaspoon cumin
- 1 teaspoon garlic powder
- 1 teaspoon paprika
- Salt and black pepper to taste
- Extra virgin olive oil

Sriracha Tahini Sauce:

- 1/4 cup tahini
- 1/4 cup water
- Juice of 1/2 lemon
- 1 tablespoon sriracha (more or less depending on your spice preference)
- Salt to taste

Optional toppings:

- Sliced avocado
- Chopped green onion
- Cilantro
- Preheat the oven to 425 degrees F.
- Place the chopped sweet potato, onion, bell pepper, and the chickpeas on a large, lined baking sheet. Drizzle with extra virgin olive oil to coat and sprinkle with cumin, garlic powder, paprika, salt and pepper. Toss with your hands to evenly coat and bake for 25-30 minutes, flipping halfway through.
- While the veggies roast, make the sriracha tahini sauce.
- Serve with any optional toppings of your choice and top with the sriracha tahini sauce.

Mexican Breakfast Tostadas

(Vegetarian)

Recipe makes 6 tostadas

- 100% corn tortillas (at least 6)
- 1 15 oz can refried beans, heated
- 1/2 cup queso fresca, crumbled
- 6 large eggs
- 2 cups pico de gallo
- 1 tablespoon extra virgin olive oil, or olive oil cooking spray

Optional toppings:

- Sliced avocado
- Chopped cilantro
- Hot sauce or salsa

1. Preheat oven to 400 degrees F.
2. Line a large baking sheet with parchment paper and place the 6 tortillas. Brush each side of the tortillas with olive oil then bake for 10-12 minutes, flipping halfway through.
3. Cook the eggs in a nonstick pan any way you desire (my personal favorite is fried with a semi-soft center).
4. To assemble, spread the refried beans onto the crispy tortillas then top with the eggs, pico de gallo, and crumble the queso fresca to top.

Pumpkin Oatmeal Muffins

(Substitute Flax Eggs to make vegan)

Recipe makes 12 muffins

- 1/2 cup canned pure pumpkin
- 2 eggs
- 2 cups old fashioned oats
- 1.5 cups unsweetened almond or oat milk
- 1 teaspoon pure vanilla extract
- 2 tablespoons pure maple syrup
- 1 scoop vanilla protein powder
- 1 teaspoon baking powder
- 1 teaspoon pumpkin pie spice
- 1/2 teaspoon cinnamon
- Pinch of salt

Optional add-ins:

- Chopped walnuts or pecans
- Chia seeds
- Ground flaxseed
- Chocolate or white chocolate chips

1. Preheat the oven to 375 degrees F.
2. In a large mixing bowl, crack and whisk the eggs until smooth. Add in the rest of the ingredients and mix well, including any add-ins of your choice.
3. Line a muffin pan with cupcake liners and evenly spoon in the mixture. Bake for 20 minutes.
4. Store leftovers in the refrigerator and reheat in the oven at 350 degrees until warm.

Spinach Puffs

(Vegetarian)

Recipe makes 12 spinach puffs

- 1 sheet puff pastry, thawed
- 1 16 oz bag frozen spinach, thawed and squeezed to remove liquid
- 6 oz crumbled feta cheese
- 1/2 cup green onions, finely chopped
- 2 teaspoons minced garlic
- Salt and black pepper to taste
- 2 large eggs, divided
- Nonstick cooking spray

1. Preheat the oven to 400 degrees F. Spray a standard 12 count muffin tin with cooking spray and set aside.

2. Roll out the puff pastry sheet with a rolling pin and cut into 12 square pieces. The dough is easily divided into 3 long strips, then cut 4 squares from each strip. Press each square piece of dough into the greased muffin tin making sure to leave the corners draped over the edge and set aside.

3. In a mixing bowl, combine the spinach, feta cheese, green onion, garlic, salt and pepper and mix well. Crack 1 egg into the mixture and stir. *It's important to squeeze as much liquid from the spinach as possible to ensure the mixture isn't soggy.

4. Evenly spoon the spinach mixture into each cavity of dough in the muffin tin then fold the four corners of the dough over the top to the center and pinch together.

5. In a separate bowl, crack the remaining egg and add 1 tablespoon of water and whisk well.

6. Brush the tops of each spinach puff with the egg wash then bake for 20 minutes, or until golden brown.

Maple Pumpkin Oat Bars

(Vegetarian; Vegan if egg is substituted for flax egg)

Recipe makes one 9x9 pan, usually cut into 9 bars

- 1/2 cup pure pumpkin puree (not pumpkin pie filling)
- 1/2 cup pure maple syrup
- 1 cup unsweetened almond or oat milk
- 1 egg
- 1/4 cup coconut oil, melted
- 1.5 cups old fashioned oats
- 1 cup oat flour (simply pulse old fashioned oats in a blender until it becomes flour-like)
- 1 teaspoon pure vanilla extract
- 1 teaspoon pumpkin pie spice
- 1 teaspoon cinnamon
- 1/2 teaspoon baking powder
- 1/2 teaspoon baking soda
- 2 tablespoons chia seeds
- Pinch of salt
- 1/2 cup chopped pecans or walnuts

1. Preheat oven to 350 degrees F.
2. Spray a 9x9 baking pan with nonstick cooking spray and set aside.
3. In a large mixing bowl, combine the milk, pumpkin, maple syrup, egg, vanilla extract and coconut oil and stir well.
4. Next, add the dry ingredients to the wet ingredients. Add in the oats, oat flour, pumpkin pie spice, cinnamon, salt, baking powder, baking soda, chia seeds, and pecans and mix well.
5. Pour the batter into the greased baking dish and even out with a spoon.
6. Bake for 35 minutes and enjoy warm.

Zucchini Squash & Corn Goat Cheese Quiche

(Vegetarian)

- 1 refrigerated pie crust (or you can omit and go crustless!)
- 1 small zucchini, thinly sliced
- 1 small squash, thinly sliced
- 1 cup of whole kernel corn
- 6 oz crumbled goat cheese
- 6 large eggs
- 1/2 cup unsweetened almond milk
- 2 tablespoons chopped basil (or sub spinach)
- 1 teaspoon lemon zest
- Salt and black pepper to taste
- Red pepper flakes, optional for heat

1. Preheat oven to 375 degrees F.
2. Press the pie crust into a 9 inch pie pan.
3. Mix all ingredients together in a large mixing bowl except for the lemon zest and pour into the pie pan onto the crust.
4. Sprinkle the lemon zest on top and bake for 30-35 minutes, or until crust is golden and egg is fully cooked.

Lemon Banana Chia Seed Muffins

(Vegetarian; Substitute Flax Eggs to make vegan)

- 2 ripe bananas,
- 2 eggs
- 1/3 cup coconut oil, melted
- 1 teaspoon vanilla extract
- 1 1/2 teaspoons lemon extract
- 1/4 cup pure maple syrup
- 1/4 cup coconut flour
- 2 cups almond flour
- 2 tablespoons chia seeds
- 1 teaspoon baking soda
- 1 teaspoon baking powder
- Pinch of salt

1. Preheat oven to 350 degrees.
2. In a large mixing bowl, mash the bananas well with a fork. Add in the wet ingredients and mix well.
3. Next, add the dry ingredients to the wet ingredients and stir to combine.
4. Evenly pour the mixture into a lined muffin tin and bake for 15-20 minutes.

Spinach Banana Protein Pancakes

(Substitute Flax Eggs to make vegan)

Recipe makes approx. 6 pancakes

- 2 cups oats
- 1 scoop vanilla protein powder
- 2 eggs
- 2 cups fresh spinach
- 1 cup oat or almond milk
- 2 teaspoons baking powder
- 1/2 teaspoon cinnamon
- 1 teaspoon vanilla extract
- 2 bananas, very ripe

Peanut butter topping:

- 3 heaping spoonfuls of peanut butter
- 1/3 cup water (you may need to add more depending on the thickness of your peanut butter)
- 1 tablespoon maple syrup (or honey for non-vegan)
- 1/2 teaspoon cinnamon, or more to taste
- 1/2 teaspoon extra virgin olive oil or coconut oil, melted

1. Start by pulsing the oats in a blender until it makes a flour-like consistency.

2. Next, add all of the other ingredients to the oats in the blender and blend together until smooth.

3. Heat extra virgin olive oil or coconut oil in a large non-stick pan over medium high heat. When oil is hot, evenly pour 1/2 cup of the pancake mix into the pan and cook until edges and bottom start to brown. Flip and repeat for the other side.

4. For the peanut butter topping, mix all ingredients together in a small bowl until smooth and creamy. You can top with any nut butter of your choice, pure maple syrup or fresh fruit.

Blueberry Coconut Chia Pudding V+

(Vegan)

Recipe makes 2 servings

- 1 15 oz can lite coconut milk
- 1/4 cup water
- 1 teaspoon vanilla extract
- 6 tablespoons chia seeds
- 2 teaspoons pure maple syrup
- 1 1/2 cups fresh or frozen blueberries

1. In a large mixing bowl, add the coconut milk, vanilla extract, maple syrup, 1/4 cup water and chia seeds.

2. Mix together and place in the refrigerator to chill for at least 6 hours to overnight.

3. Prepare the blueberry sauce by adding the blueberries and 2 tablespoons of water to a saucepan over medium heat. After about 3-5 minuets the blueberries will begin to burst. Smash them down with the back of a spoon then reduce the heat to simmer.

4. Simmer for about 10 minutes, stirring often. Remove from the saucepan and allow to cool.

5. Store the blueberry sauce in a container and refrigerate. Layer with the chia seeds in a glass or jar once ready to eat.

No-Bake Peanut Butter Protein Cookies V+

(Vegan)

Recipe makes 6 cookies

- 3/4 cup creamy peanut butter
- 1 cup oats
- 3 tablespoons pure maple syrup (or honey for non-vegan)
- 3 tablespoons chia seeds
- 1 teaspoon pure vanilla extract

1. Combine the peanut butter, syrup and vanilla extract in a bowl and microwave for 20-30 seconds.

2. Once heated and creamy, add in the rest of the ingredients plus whatever add-ins you would like. Chocolate chips, crushed almonds, walnuts or pecans, dried fruit bits, seeds, cinnamon - the options are endless!

3. Form balls with the mixture using your hands, then place onto a baking sheet lined with parchment paper and press down to make a cookie shape.

4. Refrigerate or freeze until firm and enjoy!

Creamy Baked Spinach & Eggs With Feta

(Vegetarian)

Recipe makes 4 servings

- 4 eggs
- 12 oz frozen spinach
- 1/4 cup grated parmesan cheese
- 3 oz crumbled feta cheese
- 2 tablespoons butter
- 2 tablespoons all purpose flour
- 2 teaspoons minced garlic
- 1.5 cups unsweetened almond or oat milk
- 1/2 teaspoon salt
- 1/2 teaspoon freshly cracked black pepper
- Pinch of paprika
- Red pepper flakes (optional)
- Toasted sourdough bread (optional for dipping)

1. Preheat the oven to 400 degrees F.

2. Melt the butter in a skillet over medium heat and add in the minced garlic, sautéing for about 1 minute. Whisk the flour into the melted butter and continue stirring for about 2 minutes. The butter and flour should form a paste and will start to bubble as it cooks.

3. Slowly pour in the milk and whisk with the flour and butter paste. Mix well until there are no lumps. Add in the salt, black pepper, and paprika.

4. Continuing to whisk, allow the milk come to a simmer. Once it starts to thicken, add in the parmesan cheese and stir.

5. Add in the frozen spinach and continue cooking until heated through and fully thawed, about 5 minutes. Taste and add more salt/pepper if needed.

6. Using a spoon, create 4 pockets in the spinach and crack one egg into each. Don't worry if the egg whites run outside of the pockets a bit.

7. Sprinkle crumbled feta over the entire dish and bake for 15 minutes.

8. Serve hot with some crispy, toasted bread and enjoy!

Spanakopita - Greek Spinach & Feta Pies

(Vegetarian)

Recipe makes approx. 20 hand pies

- One 16 oz box phyllo dough, thawed
- Two 12 oz packages frozen spinach, thawed and squeezed to remove water
- 1/2 white onion, finely diced
- 6-7 green onions, chopped
- .5 oz fresh dill, chopped
- 8 oz block of feta cheese
- 1 egg, lightly beaten
- 1 tablespoon minced garlic
- 1 teaspoon salt
- 1 teaspoon cracked black pepper
- 1 tablespoon extra virgin olive oil
- 2-3 tablespoons butter, melted

1. Transfer the spinach to a large mixing bowl, making sure to squeeze out the water. It's important to squeeze out as much water as possible to make sure the filling isn't too wet.

2. Heat the olive oil in a nonstick pan over medium heat. When the oil is hot, add the white and green onions and sauté for about 3-4 minutes. Next, add in the minced garlic and the dill and continue to cook for another 3 minutes. Add to the spinach in the mixing bowl and stir to combine.

3. Using your hands, crumble the feta cheese block into the spinach mixture, add salt and pepper and mix well to combine.

4. Crack the egg into a small bowl and whisk or lightly beat with a fork then pour into spinach mixture and mix well.

5. Preheat oven to 375 degrees.

6. Place a sheet of parchment paper onto your countertop for the assembly station, then transfer 3 stacked sheets of the phyllo dough onto the parchment paper at a time. Using a pizza cutter, cut the phyllo dough sheets in half, lengthwise. Every 3 sheets of phyllo dough will make 2 pies.

7. Spoon about 2 heaping spoonfuls of the spinach mixture onto the end of the phyllo dough and then fold the left corner over to the right side, forming a triangle. Continue folding the dough over, keeping the triangular shape until you have formed the pie.

8. Arrange the pies on a lined baking sheet. Once all of the pies are made and on the baking sheet, melt the butter in a small bowl in the microwave. Using a pastry brush, brush the butter onto both sides of the pies and bake for 25-30 minutes, or until golden brown.

9. Serve immediately. You can store the leftovers in the fridge and reheat by rebaking them in the oven at 350 degrees, until hot.

Mains

Super Green Buddha Bowl

(Vegan)

Recipe makes approx. 4 servings

- 1 crown of broccoli, chopped into florets
- 1/2 bundle of fresh asparagus, ends removed and chopped into pieces about 2 inches long
- 1 cup frozen peas
- 2 avocados, halved and sliced
- 1 cup wild rice or quinoa
- 4 cups fresh spinach
- One 12 oz. container of hummus
- 1 lemon
- 4 tablespoons tahini (more or less depending on personal preference)
- 4 teaspoons pesto, homemade or store bought
- 2 teaspoons minced garlic
- Salt and black pepper to taste
- Red chili flakes (optional for heat)
- 2 tablespoons extra virgin olive oil

1. Start by cooking the wild rice or quinoa according to package directions.

2. While the rice/quinoa is cooking, heat the olive oil in a large nonstick pan over medium high heat, then add the broccoli and asparagus and sauté until the veggies start to get slightly browned. Add in the frozen peas, minced garlic, salt and pepper and continue cooking for another few minutes, or until the peas are cooked through.

3. To assemble the bowls, start by placing 1 cup of fresh spinach in a bowl, then place about 2 heaping spoonfuls of rice or quinoa in the center on the bed of spinach. Next add the broccoli, asparagus, peas, and the slices of 1/2 of an avocado. Top with a heaping spoonful of hummus and 1 teaspoon of pesto, then drizzle 1 tablespoon of tahini. Squeeze the juice of 1 lemon wedge over the bowl and sprinkle with red chili flakes if desired.

Oven Roasted Honey Cinnamon Pear & Brussel Sprouts Salad

(Vegetarian; Vegan if goat cheese is omitted)

Recipe makes about 4 servings

- 1 20 oz bag cubed butternut squash
- 1 16 oz bag brussel sprouts, chopped into halves
- 1 fresh whole garlic
- 2 slightly ripe pears (Anjou or Bartlett pears work best)
- 1/2 of 1 red onion, chopped into pieces about 1 inch
- 2 cups fresh kale, chopped
- 1 teaspoon pure maple syrup (or honey for non-vegan option)
- Pinch of cinnamon
- 1 teaspoon salt
- 1 teaspoon black pepper
- Sliced almonds and dried cranberries for topping
- Crumbled goat cheese
- Balsamic glaze, to top
- Extra virgin olive oil

1. Start by preheating the oven to 375 degrees.
2. Line a large baking sheet and place the butternut squash on one half and the brussel sprouts on the other.
3. Remove the garlic pods from the bulb and chop off both end pieces to the pods while leaving the skin on. Add the red onion and garlic to the baking sheet with the squash and brussels. Drizzle olive oil onto the vegetables, sprinkle with salt and pepper and toss to combine. Set aside.
4. Dice the pears by chopping off the stem first, then cutting in half lengthwise. Be sure to remove the seeds and the hard part in the center before dicing into cubes.
5. Place the diced pears into an 8x8 baking dish, drizzle a small amount of olive oil (about 1 teaspoon), 1 teaspoon of honey or syrup and a pinch of cinnamon. Toss to combine.
6. Roast the pears and vegetables at the same time for 30 minutes, flipping halfway through.
7. When vegetables and pears have about 5-10 minutes left to roast, sauté the chopped kale with olive oil in a large skillet and set aside.
8. Remove vegetables and pears from oven when roasting is complete and peel and remove skin from the garlic pods.
9. Mix all vegetables with the pear and kale to assemble the salad. Top with balsamic glaze, sliced almonds, dried cranberries and crumbled goat cheese.

Mean Green Avocado Pesto Pasta With Truffle Oil

(Vegetarian)

Recipe makes approx. 6 servings

Pasta:

- 1 16 oz. package rigatoni pasta
- 1 zucchini, sliced
- 1/2 bundle of fresh asparagus, chopped
- 1 cup frozen peas
- 2 cups fresh spinach
- Extra virgin olive oil
- Grated white cheese (optional, for topping)

Avocado Truffle Pesto Sauce:

- 1 avocado
- Juice of 1 lime
- 2 handfuls fresh spinach
- 3-4 tablespoons pesto, homemade or store bought
- 2/3 cup unsweetened dairy free milk
- 1 garlic clove or 1 teaspoon minced garlic
- 1 teaspoon Italian herbs seasoning
- 1 teaspoon salt
- 1/2 teaspoon cracked black pepper
- 1 teaspoon truffle oil
- Red pepper flakes, optional for heat

1. Cook pasta according to package directions.
2. While the pasta is cooking, make the avocado truffle pesto sauce by combining all ingredients in a blender or food processor until smooth. If it's too thick, continue to add more milk or water in small amounts until desired consistency is reached. Set aside.
3. Heat the olive oil over medium heat in a large nonstick pan then add the zucchini and asparagus. Cook until soft and slightly browned then add in the peas and continue cooking until the peas get soft and turn bright green. Next, add in the spinach and cook until it starts to wilt.
4. Pour the sauce over the vegetables and mix to combine, then serve over the pasta.
5. Add shredded or crumbled white cheese of your choice to top if desired. I like fontina, feta or goat cheese the best with this dish!

Spinach & Mushroom Cheesy Cauliflower Crust Calzones

(Vegetarian)

Recipe makes 4 calzones

- 1 extra large head of cauliflower, or 2 smaller ones (you'll need enough to make 6 cups of cauliflower rice)
- 1.5 cups sliced baby bella (cremini) mushrooms
- 4 cups fresh spinach
- 8 oz. shredded mozzarella cheese
- 4 teaspoons pesto, store bought or homemade
- 4 tablespoons alfredo pasta sauce, store bought or homemade
- 2 teaspoons minced garlic
- 1 teaspoon Italian seasoning
- 1 teaspoon salt
- 1/2 teaspoon cracked black pepper
- 1 egg
- 1 tablespoon olive oil

1. Preheat the oven to 450 degrees F and line a baking sheet with parchment paper, grease it with olive oil or cooking spray and set aside.

2. Chop the cauliflower into small florets and pulse in a blender or food processor as if it were a rice-like consistency. You want it to be evenly chopped and not completely smooth.

3. Heat the olive oil in a pot over medium high heat, then add the cauliflower rice and stir to combine with the oil. Cover with the lid and let it cook and steam for about 10 minutes, stirring every couple of minutes.

4. Once cooked, remove from heat and let cool. When it's cooled enough to hold with your hands, add the cauliflower rice in batches into a tea towel and squeeze out as much of the liquid as possible. Do not skip this step! The cauliflower needs to be as dry as possible, otherwise the dough will be mushy and it will not hold together. I usually squeeze out about 1 cup of liquid.

5. Transfer the cauliflower to a large mixing bowl and add in the lightly beaten egg, 1/2 cup of mozzarella cheese, Italian seasoning, salt and pepper and mix well.

6. Using your hands, press the mixture onto the baking sheet and form the crusts, using 1.5 cups of cauliflower rice for each. They should be about 5 inches in diameter. Place in the oven on the middle rack and bake for exactly 10 minutes. Do not over or under cook!

7. While the crusts are baking, heat olive oil in a nonstick pan over medium heat. Add the mushrooms and sauté for about 5 minutes, then add the spinach and minced garlic and cook until the spinach starts to wilt.

8. Remove the crusts from the oven and spoon 1 tablespoon of Alfredo and 1 teaspoon of pesto onto each crust (you can add more if you'd like.) Next add some mozzarella cheese to only half of each crust, then place the mushrooms and spinach on top of the cheese, and sprinkle a little more cheese on top of the mushrooms and spinach. Carefully fold the half of the crust with no filling over the half with the filling using a large spatula to make the calzones. Don't worry if the crust breaks a bit. You can just press it back into shape using your fingers.

9. Place back in the oven and bake for an additional 10-12 minutes and serve warm.

Sri Lankan Kottu

(Vegetarian; Vegan if egg is omitted)

Recipe makes approx. 6 servings

- 1/2 red onion, chopped into strips
- 1/2 head green cabbage, chopped into strips
- 4 green onions, chopped
- 1 cup shredded carrot
- 1 serrano or jalapeno pepper, seeded and finely chopped
- 4 pieces of roti, chapati, or paratha
- 1 tablespoon minced garlic
- 1 inch piece of ginger, grated
- 1 cup canned coconut milk
- 2 eggs
- 1 tablespoon tomato paste
- 1 tablespoon yellow curry powder
- 1 teaspoon cumin
- 1 teaspoon chili powder
- Salt and black pepper to taste
- 2 tablespoons olive oil

1. Heat the olive oil in a wok or pot over medium heat. Add the ginger, garlic and serrano or jalapeños and sauté for a few minutes, until fragrant. Next, add in the red onion, cabbage, carrots, and green onion and sauté for about 5 more minutes.

2. Add the tomato paste and all seasonings in with the vegetables and continue to sauté until fully coated. Pour in the coconut milk and mix well.

3. In a separate bowl, crack the eggs and lightly beat with a fork. Move the vegetables over to one side of the wok and pour in the eggs to scramble. Once scrambled, mix in with the rest of the curry.

4. Cut the roti into strips and mix in with the vegetable curry. Serve hot.

Spinach Lasagna Roll-Ups

(Vegetarian)

Recipe makes 10 lasagna rolls

- 1 lb. beyond meat plant based crumbles (if you're a meat eater, you can use 1 lb. lean ground turkey)
- 16 oz package of lasagna noodles
- 1 24 oz can of tomato pasta sauce
- 15 oz low fat ricotta cheese
- 2 cups shredded mozzarella cheese, divided
- 2-3 cups fresh spinach, chopped
- 2 tablespoons minced garlic
- 1 teaspoon garlic powder
- 1 teaspoon onion powder
- 1 teaspoon Italian seasoning or oregano
- 1 teaspoon salt
- 1 teaspoon black pepper
- Red pepper flakes, optional for heat
- Fresh basil or parsley, optional for topping

1. Preheat the oven to 350 degrees F.

2. Boil the lasagna noodles according to package directions, being careful not to overcook or tear them.

3. While the noodles boil, cook the meat crumbles in a non-stick pan over medium heat for about 5 minutes, then add the minced garlic and cook for another 2 minutes. Transfer to a large mixing bowl when finished cooking and add the ricotta cheese, chopped spinach, garlic powder, onion powder, salt, pepper, red pepper flakes, Italian seasoning, and 1 cup of shredded mozzarella cheese. Mix well.

4. When the noodles finish cooking, drain them and rinse with cool water. Next, lay them out flat on the counter on a sheet of parchment paper. You will use this as your rolling station.

5. Pour enough of the tomato pasta sauce into a 5 quart casserole dish to cover the bottom. I usually use a little less than half of the sauce.

6. Next, spoon the lasagna filling onto the noodles and then roll the noodles all the way up. Place the rolls seam down onto the pasta sauce in the baking dish and repeat.

7. Pour the remaining pasta sauce over the tops of the lasagna rolls and top with 1 cup of mozzarella cheese.

8. Bake uncovered for 20-25 minutes and then garnish with chopped parsley or basil.

Green Goddess Pizza

(Vegetarian)

Recipe makes one 14-16 inch pizza

- 1 lb. ready to bake refrigerated pizza dough, thin crust or rolled out to be thin crust. (My personal favorite is the pizza dough from Trader Joe's)
- 1/3 cup Alfredo sauce, store bought or home made
- 2 tablespoons pesto, store bought or home made
- 1 zucchini, thinly sliced
- 1 12 oz can quartered artichokes, drained
- 1-2 handfuls fresh baby spinach
- 8 oz fontina cheese, grated
- 4 oz. cremini mushrooms (baby bella), sliced
- 4 oz. crumbled feta or goat cheese (or add both!)
- 1 handful fresh arugula (optional, for topping after baking)

1. Preheat the oven to 425 degrees F.

2. Slice the zucchini into thin slices then transfer to a mixing bowl. Add the pesto to the zucchini and mix well to coat both sides of the zucchini slices. Set aside.

3. On a floured surface, roll out the pizza dough then transfer to a lined, greased 16" pizza pan.

4. Add the Alfredo sauce to the dough, spreading evenly, then top with the grated fontina cheese. I usually add enough cheese to cover the sauce.

5. Place the pesto zucchini slices all around the pizza then top with the spinach, mushrooms and artichokes (I usually use about 1/2 of the can of artichokes).

6. Add a little more of the grated fontina cheese to lightly top the veggies, then top with feta/goat cheese crumbles.

7. Bake for 20 minutes, checking around 15 minutes since ovens typically vary, and cook until you get your desired crust.

8. After the pizza is cooked, remove from oven and top with red pepper flakes and fresh arugula (optional).

Rainbow Buddha Bowls With Cilantro Lime Sauce

(Vegan)

Recipe makes approx 4 servings

- 1 red bell pepper, chopped
- 1 yellow bell pepper, chopped
- 1 crown of broccoli, chopped into florets
- 2 cups matchstick carrots
- 2 cups red cabbage, chopped
- 1 cup quinoa or brown rice
- 2 avocados, halved and sliced
- 2 tablespoons extra virgin olive oil

Cilantro Lime Sauce:

- 1 avocado
- 1/2 bunch of cilantro, stems are ok to add
- Juice of 1 lime
- 5 oz plain vegan yogurt (use plain greek yogurt for non-vegan option)
- 1 jalapeno, seeded and chopped into pieces about 1 inch
- 1 tablespoon minced garlic
- 1 teaspoon salt
- 1 teaspoon black pepper

1. Cook the quinoa or brown rice according to package directions.

2. While the quinoa cooks, make the cilantro lime sauce by combining all ingredients in a blender or food processor and blending until smooth. If the sauce is a bit too thick, just add water in small increments and blend until you reach your desired consistency. Set aside.

3. Heat the olive oil in a large nonstick pan over medium heat. Add the broccoli and bell peppers and sauté for about 8 minutes or until vegetables start to get soft. You do not need to cook the carrots and red cabbage! Just add them to the bowl fresh.

4. To assemble the bowls, spoon the quinoa into the center of the bowl, then plate the veggies all around it. Add the sliced avocado with the bowls and top with the cilantro lime sauce and enjoy!

Summer Quinoa Salad

(Vegetarian)

Recipe makes approx. 4 servings

- One 15 oz can chickpeas, drained and rinsed
- One 8 oz can corn, drained and rinsed
- 1/2 cup quinoa, uncooked
- 1 avocado, diced
- 2 roma tomatoes, diced
- 3 green onions, chopped
- Handful of fresh dill, chopped
- Crumbled feta cheese, to top

Dressing:

- Juice of 1 lemon
- Juice of 1 lime
- 1 tablespoon olive oil
- 1 teaspoon minced garlic
- 1 teaspoon salt
- 1 teaspoon black pepper

1. Cook the quinoa on the stovetop or in a rice cooker, according to package directions.
2. While the quinoa is cooking, combine all of the ingredients for the salad in a large mixing bowl. Add the quinoa once its finished cooking.
3. Mix all of the ingredients for the dressing together in a small bowl, then pour over the salad and toss to combine. Refrigerate any leftovers and enjoy cold or at room temperature.

Korean BBQ Jackfruit Tacos

(Vegan)

Recipe makes approx 12 tacos

- 12 corn tortillas
- Two 20oz cans jackfruit
- Red cabbage, chopped
- Matchstick carrots
- Cucumber, sliced
- 1 lime
- Cilantro, chopped
- 1 jalapeno or serrano pepper, chopped (optional for heat)

Korean BBQ sauce:

- 1/4 cup soy sauce
- 1/3 cup pure maple syrup
- 1 tablespoon rice vinegar
- Pinch of cayenne pepper
- 1 teaspoon ground ginger
- 1 teaspoon minced garlic
- 1 tablespoon corn starch + 1 tablespoon water

1. Rinse and drain the jackfruit, chop off the hard ends, and discard the big seeds.
2. Boil the jackfruit in a large pot for 30 minutes.
3. Meanwhile, make the Korean BBQ sauce by combining all ingredients in a small mixing bowl except for the cornstarch and water. Separately, mix the corn starch and water together until smooth and set aside.
4. Transfer the sauce to a saucepan and bring to a boil, then pour in the cornstarch and water mixture. Lower the heat and let simmer until the sauce thickens, then set aside.
5. Preheat the oven to 400 degrees F.
6. When the jackfruit is ready, drain and pull apart with two forks, until the jackfruit becomes stringy (similar to shredded chicken or pulled pork).
7. Add the Korean BBQ sauce to the jackfruit and toss, saving about 1 cup of the sauce for later. Transfer the jackfruit to a baking sheet lined with parchment paper and bake for 20 minutes.
8. When the jackfruit is finished cooking in the oven, add the rest of the BBQ sauce and toss.
9. Assemble the tacos with the jackfruit first and top with the fresh carrot, cabbage, cucumber, lime and cilantro.

Thai Butternut Squash Curry

(Vegan)

Recipe makes approx. 4 servings

- 1 bag (16 oz.) cubed butternut squash
- 3 cups fresh baby spinach
- 1 tablespoon ginger, peeled and finely chopped
- 1 teaspoon ground turmeric
- 1 teaspoon garlic powder
- 1 teaspoon curry powder
- 1/2 teaspoon red pepper flakes
- 1 large shallot, diced
- 1 can (15 oz.) lite coconut milk
- 2 tablespoons red curry paste
- 1 cup low sodium vegetable broth
- 1 cup jasmine or basmati rice, uncooked
- 1 tablespoon coconut oil
- Dash of salt and black pepper to taste
- Chopped cilantro and crushed peanuts (for topping; optional)

1. Cook the rice according to package directions.

2. In a large nonstick saucepan heat the coconut oil over medium heat and add the shallots once hot. Cook for about 5 minutes, or until shallots begin to get golden.

3. Add in the butternut squash, ginger, garlic powder, turmeric, curry powder and curry paste and mix well. Continue cooking for a few minutes, until fragrant.

4. Add the vegetable broth, coconut milk, red pepper flakes, salt and pepper and let the sauce come to a simmer before covering with the lid.

5. Lower the heat and let simmer for about 15 minutes, allowing the squash to cook all the way through.

6. Stir in the spinach until wilted and serve over warm rice. Top with cilantro and/or crushed peanuts

Cauliflower Rice Taco Bowls With Chipotle Lime Ranch (V+)

(Vegan)

Recipe makes approx 6 servings

Taco Bowl:

- 1 large head of cauliflower, chopped into florets
- 1/2 red onion, diced
- 1 red bell pepper, chopped
- 1 15 oz can black beans, drained and rinsed
- 1 jalapeños, seeded and diced
- 1 tablespoon minced garlic
- 2 teaspoons cumin
- 1 teaspoon chili powder
- 1 teaspoon smoked paprika
- Salt and black pepper to taste
- Extra virgin olive oil
- Smashed avocado, cilantro, & freshly squeezed lime juice, optional for topping

Chipotle Lime Ranch:

- 8 oz vegan ranch dressing
- 1-2 canned chipotle peppers and 2 tablespoons of adobo sauce (from the can)
- 1 cup cilantro
- Juice of 1 lime
- 1 tablespoon minced garlic
- 1 teaspoon onion powder
- 1/2 teaspoon smoked paprika
- Salt and black pepper

1. Make the chipotle lime ranch by adding all ingredients to a blender and blending until smooth. Pour in a small bowl or container and place in the refrigerator until the taco bowls are ready.

2. To make the taco bowls, first add the cauliflower florets into a blender or food processor and pulse until it makes a rice consistency. You may need to do this in batches. Set aside.

3. Heat the olive oil in a large pot over medium heat. When hot, add the red onion, bell pepper, and jalapeño and cook for a few minutes. Next, add the minced garlic and seasonings and cook for another minute or so, until fragrant.

4. Add the black beans and cauliflower rice and stir until mixed well. You may need to adjust the seasonings a bit and salt here.

5. When plated, drizzle the chipotle lime ranch over the top and add smashed avocado, cilantro and lime juice to top if desired.

Honey Sriracha Cauliflower

(Vegetarian; Vegan if honey is substituted with agave)

Recipe makes approx. 4 servings

- 1 large head of cauliflower
- 2 - 3 tablespoons sriracha (more or less depending on how spicy you like it)
- 5 tablespoons low sodium soy sauce
- 1 tablespoon minced garlic
- 1/4 cup sugar
- 2 tablespoons honey or agave
- 2 tablespoons corn starch
- 1 cup brown or jasmine rice
- 1 cup water
- Chopped green onion (optional)

1. Chop the cauliflower into florets and add to a large sauce pan or pot with extra virgin olive oil over medium heat and sauté for about 15 minutes or until tender, stirring often.

2. While the cauliflower is cooking, make the sauce by combining 1 cup of water, soy sauce, minced garlic, sriracha, agave/honey and sugar in a small sauce pan or pot. Bring to a boil over medium heat.

3. In a separate bowl, mix 2 tablespoons of corn starch and 2 tablespoons of water together until dissolved and pour into the sauce. Stir until thickened and then reduce the heat to low.

4. Pour the sauce over the cooked cauliflower and stir to coat.

5. Serve over rice and top with chopped green onion.

Better Than Takeout Vegetable Fried Rice

(Vegetarian; Vegan if egg is omitted)

Recipe makes approx. 6 servings

- 1 cup brown rice, cooked
- 1 cup cauliflower florets
- 1 cup broccoli florets
- 1 cup portobello or shiitake mushrooms, chopped
- 2 cups mixed frozen peas and carrots
- 1 tablespoon minced garlic
- 1/2 white onion, chopped
- 2 green onions, chopped
- 1 cup fresh baby spinach, chopped
- 3 eggs
- 2 tablespoons low sodium soy sauce
- 2 tablespoons sesame seed oil
- 1 teaspoon ground ginger
- 1 tablespoon sriracha or 1 teaspoon red pepper flakes (more or less, depending on your desired spice level)
- Salt and black pepper to taste

1. Start by heating the sesame oil in a large pot over medium high heat, then add the onions and sauté for about 3 minutes.

2. Next, add the minced garlic and ground ginger to the onion and continue to cook for another 2 minutes.

3. Add in the cauliflower and broccoli florets and continue cooking until veggies start to soften.

4. While the veggies are cooking, crack the 3 eggs in a small bowl and whisk with a fork until yolks are combined with the egg whites. Set aside.

5. Next, add the frozen peas and carrots, mushrooms and spinach and continue cooking all the vegetables together until the frozen veggies are cooked through.

6. When the veggies are fully cooked, push them all over to one side of the pot and pour the egg mixture to scramble. You can also scramble the eggs in a separate nonstick pan and then add to the veggies if you'd prefer.

7. When the eggs are finished cooking, add in the cooked rice, green onion, sriracha or red pepper flakes and stir well to combine. Add salt and black pepper to taste and serve immediately.

Sesame Ginger Soba Noodles

(Vegan)

Recipe makes approx. 4 servings

- One 14 oz. package soba noodles
- 1 large red bell pepper, sliced
- 2 cups shredded carrot
- 2 cups chopped red cabbage
- 2 cups frozen shelled edamame, thawed
- 1 bunch green onions, chopped
- 2 tablespoons almond butter
- 2 tablespoons rice vinegar
- 2 tablespoons toasted sesame seed oil
- 1 tablespoon low sodium soy sauce or tamari
- 1 teaspoon ground ginger
- 1-2 teaspoons sriracha or chili paste (optional for heat)
- Juice of 1/2 lime

Optional garnish:

- Sesame seeds

1. Start by cooking the soba noodles according to package directions.
2. While the noodles boil, make the sesame ginger sauce by combining the almond butter, rice vinegar, soy sauce or tamari, sesame oil, ground ginger, lime juice and sriracha or chili paste in a small bowl. If the sauce is too thick, add water in small increments until desired consistency is reached.
3. When the noodles are ready, drain and rinse with cool water, then plate and toss with the sesame ginger sauce. Arrange with the carrots, red peppers, edamame, red cabbage and green onions and garnish with sesame seeds if desired.

Brussel Sprout, Butternut Squash & Crispy Potato Tacos

(Vegetarian; Vegan if cheese & spicy mayo are omitted)

Recipe makes 8-10 tacos. Serving size is usually about 2-3 tacos per person.

- 1 lb. brussel sprouts
- 1 medium - large russet potato, peeled and diced
- 1/2 red onion, chopped
- 1 10 oz bag of cubed butternut squash
- 1 can refried black beans
- 1 lime
- 1/2 red onion, diced
- 1 pack of corn tortillas
- 1 teaspoon cumin
- 1/2 teaspoon cayenne pepper
- 1/2 teaspoon turmeric
- 1/2 teaspoon curry powder
- 1/2 teaspoon paprika
- 2 teaspoons garlic powder
- Salt and black pepper to taste
- Extra virgin olive oil

Optional toppings:

- Goat cheese
- Spicy mayo (you can find this in most grocery stores in the Asian section)
- Chopped cilantro

I personally don't find spicy mayo very spicy, but if you want a milder flavor you can use garlic aioli, pesto, or chimichurri instead.

1. Preheat the oven to 375 degrees F and line a baking sheet with parchment paper or foil.
2. Chop the ends off of the brussel sprouts, cut into halves or quarters then place on a lined baking sheet (This should take up about half of the baking sheet). Next, empty the bag of cubed butter-

nut squash onto the baking sheet to take up the other half. Drizzle olive oil over the vegetables (you want to use enough oil to coat all of the veggies without completely drenching them). Sprinkle with salt, black pepper, and garlic powder. Toss with your hands to evenly coat the veggies in oil and seasonings.

3. Bake for 30 minutes, flipping halfway through.

4. While the veggies are roasting in the oven, start pan frying the potatoes to get them nice and crispy. Heat olive oil in a non-stick pan over medium heat. Add the diced potatoes and sauté for about 2-3 minutes, ensuring to coat all sides of the potatoes in oil. Add the cumin, curry powder, turmeric, paprika, garlic powder, cayenne pepper, and salt and pepper. Toss evenly to coat the potatoes in the seasonings. To really get the potatoes nice and crispy, you'll need to let each side of the potatoes sit and cook in the oil by only flipping occasionally. It usually takes me about 15 minutes to really get them cooked through and crispy. Set aside when finished cooking.

5. When using corn tortillas I find that wrapping about 6 of them in a paper towel and microwaving for about 30-40 seconds really helps to make them pliable. Then I like to heat them in a pan over medium heat to make them slightly golden and charred around the edges. This step can be skipped, but who doesn't love a warm, golden, crisp tortilla?!

6. To assemble the tacos, spread 1 or 2 spoonfuls of refried black beans onto the tortilla, then add the potato, squash, and brussel sprouts. Top with diced red onion and chopped cilantro and add spicy mayo (or your preferred sauce) and some crumbled goat cheese. Squeeze some fresh lime juice to top it all off.

Vegetarian Mexican Burritos

(Vegetarian)

Recipe makes a lot LOL

- 1 15 oz can black beans, drained and rinsed
- 1 15 oz can refried black beans
- 1 orange or yellow bell pepper, chopped
- 1 tomato, diced
- 1 small red onion, diced
- 1 jalapeno, diced
- 1 cup uncooked quinoa (sub brown rice)
- Shredded Mexican cheese
- 1/2 bunch cilantro, chopped
- 2 teaspoons cumin
- 1 teaspoon chili powder
- 1 teaspoon paprika
- 1 teaspoon garlic powder
- Salt and black pepper to taste
- 1/2 teaspoon cayenne pepper
- 10 large burrito style tortillas

For guacamole:

- 2 avocados
- Juice of 1 lime
- Salt and pepper to taste

1. Start by cooking the quinoa in a rice cooker or in a pot on the stovetop over medium heat. Combine 1 cup dry, uncooked quinoa and 2 cups of water and cook on medium-low heat until water is absorbed and you can fluff easily with a fork.

2. While the quinoa is cooking, make the guacamole by smashing the 2 avocados in a bowl with a fork. Squeeze the juice of 1 lime and season with salt and black pepper. Set aside.

83

3. Next add the black beans, tomato, onion, bell pepper and jalapeño to a large mixing bowl with all seasonings. Add the chopped cilantro and stir well to combine.

4. When the quinoa finishes cooking, combine it with the vegetables and seasonings in the bowl and mix. Adjust seasonings if needed.

5. To assemble the burritos, start by spreading the refried black beans onto the tortilla and then spoon the filling onto the center. Top with some shredded cheese then tuck the ends in and roll the tortilla into a burrito.

6. You can enjoy as is, or heat in a pan over medium heat with a little bit of extra virgin olive oil to get the tortilla crispy and golden with melted cheese inside. Top with guacamole and enjoy!

Roasted Cauliflower Steaks With Sweet Potato Mash Ⓥ⁺

(Vegan)

Recipe makes 4-6 servings

- 1 large head of cauliflower
- 2 large sweet potatoes, peeled and chopped
- 1/2 cup of lentils, uncooked
- 1 teaspoon ground cumin
- 1 teaspoon smoked paprika
- 1 teaspoon ground turmeric
- 1/2 teaspoon cayenne (optional for heat)
- 1/2 teaspoon cinnamon
- 1/4 cup tahini
- Juice of 1 lemon

Cilantro Lime Sauce:

- 1 bunch cilantro
- Juice of 1 lime
- 3 garlic cloves
- 5 oz. plain vegan yogurt (or plain greek yogurt for non-vegan option)
- 1/2 of 1 jalapeño, seeded
- 1/2 of 1 avocado
- 1/2 teaspoon salt and black pepper

1. Preheat oven to 400 degrees F.
2. Fill a large pot with water and place over high heat to boil the sweet potatoes. Add potatoes to boiling water when ready and boil until potatoes are soft and easily pierced with a fork.
3. Cook the lentils in a medium sized pot or saucepan by combining the 1/2 cup dry lentils with 1 1/2 cups of water. Bring to a boil, cover with the lid, reduce heat and simmer until tender and water is absorbed. Typically, about 20 minutes.

4. While the potatoes and lentils cook, slice the cauliflower into steaks, about 1 inch thick, leaving the stem at the bottom. Some florets will break off and you can just roast these on the pan along with the steaks.

5. Place the cauliflower steaks on a lined baking sheet and drizzle with olive oil. Rub to coat both sides, then sprinkle with the seasonings and salt and black pepper.

6. Roast for 25 minutes, flipping halfway through.

7. When the sweet potatoes are cooked, remove from water and mash with a fork (or puree in a food processor), and then add in the cinnamon with a pinch of salt and pepper to taste.

8. To make the cilantro lime sauce, just combine all ingredients in a food processor or blender and blend until smooth. If the sauce is too thick, add a little bit of water until you reach your desired consistency.

9. To serve: Layer the mashed sweet potatoes on a plate, add a layer of lentils, place a cauliflower steak on top, and top the dish with the cilantro lime sauce and tahini. If your tahini is more on the thicker side, adding the juice of a lemon to it will make it creamier.

Teriyaki Cauliflower Grain Bowl V+

(Vegan)

Recipe makes approx 4 bowls

- 1 cup brown rice, uncooked
- 1 head cauliflower, chopped into florets
- 4 cups chopped red cabbage
- 2 cups matchstick carrots
- One 10 oz bag frozen shelled edamame, thawed
- 1 avocado
- 1 lime, cut into wedges
- Teriyaki sauce, store bought or home made
- Extra virgin olive oil
- Salt and black pepper to taste

Optional garnishes:

- Sliced green or red chilies (for spice)
- Green onion
- Sesame seeds
- Cilantro

1. Preheat the oven to 425 degrees F.

2. Cook the rice in a rice cooker or on the stovetop in a small-medium sized pot over medium heat. Lower the heat and cover with the lid until fully cooked. Once fully cooked, add in 1-2 tablespoons of teriyaki sauce and mix well.

3. Place the cauliflower florets onto a lined baking sheet and drizzle with olive oil. Sprinkle with salt and pepper and toss to evenly coat. Bake for 20 minutes, flipping halfway through, then toss with the teriyaki sauce. You should put enough sauce to fully coat the cauliflower without completely drenching them. Bake for another 5-7 minutes, until caramelized.

4. To arrange the bowls, spoon about 1/4 cup of the cooked teriyaki rice into a bowl, then add the teriyaki cauliflower florets, shredded carrot, chopped red cabbage and sliced avocado. Squeeze the juice of a lime wedge to top, and add any garnishes of your choice. You can drizzle more teriyaki sauce to top if desired.

Very Vegan Power Bowl

(Vegan)

Makes approx 4 bowls

- 1 cup quinoa, uncooked
- 1 head cauliflower, chopped into florets
- 1 crown broccoli, chopped into florets
- 4 cups fresh spinach
- 2 avocados
- 12 oz hummus (any kind you prefer)
- 4 tablespoons tahini
- 1 lemon, cut into wedges
- Extra virgin olive oil
- 2 teaspoons garlic powder
- Salt and black pepper to taste

Optional garnish:

- Chili garlic sauce or Sriracha
- Hemp seeds
- Pumpkin seeds or almond slices

1. Cook the quinoa in a small-medium sized pot over medium heat with 2 cups of water. Cover with the lid and lower the heat to simmer until cooked and easily fluffed with a fork.

2. Preheat the oven to 425 degrees F.

3. Place the cauliflower florets onto a large, lined baking sheet. Drizzle with olive oil (enough to coat without over saturating them), sprinkle with garlic powder, salt and pepper and toss evenly to coat. Bake for 20 minutes, flipping halfway through.

4. While the cauliflower is roasting, sauté the broccoli florets in a large nonstick pan with olive oil.

5. To arrange the bowls, start by making a bed of fresh spinach, then spoon some of the cooked quinoa onto the spinach, then add cauliflower and broccoli florets and top with a heaping spoonful of hummus. Top with tahini and squeeze fresh lemon juice. Add any garnishes of your choice to top.

Singapore Noodles (V+)

(Vegan)

Recipe makes approx 6 servings

- 8 oz. package of vermicelli noodles
- 1 red bell pepper, chopped into strips
- 1/2 onion, chopped into strips
- 1 cup matchstick carrots
- 1 small head of broccoli, chopped into small florets
- 1-2 cups chopped green cabbage
- 4 oz. shiitake mushrooms
- 3 green onions, chopped
- 1 tablespoon yellow curry powder
- 1 teaspoon ground turmeric
- 1 teaspoon ground ginger
- 1 teaspoon garlic powder
- 1/2 teaspoon cayenne pepper
- 3 tablespoons liquid aminos or light soy sauce
- 2 tablespoons rice wine vinegar or sherry cooking wine
- 1 tablespoon sesame seed oil
- 2-3 tablespoons vegetable oil or extra virgin olive oil

1. Heat vegetable or olive oil in a large wok or pot over medium heat. When oil is hot add the broccoli, bell pepper, onion, carrots, mushrooms and cabbage and sauté for about 5 minutes then lower the heat and continue to stir occasionally.

2. Meanwhile, cook the noodles according to package directions. It does not take long to boil vermicelli noodles!

3. After the noodles are cooked, drain and combine with the vegetables. Add the liquid aminos, rice wine vinegar, sesame seed oil and all seasonings and mix well to combine. Chop the noodles with your mixing spoon while mixing to cut them into smaller pieces. You can also adjust the spices if needed to your desired preference.

4. Plate in a bowl and enjoy hot. Top with chopped green onion.

Japanese Udon Noodles

(Vegan)

Recipe makes approx. 4 servings

- 1 14 oz package of Udon noodles
- 2 cups broccoli, chopped into small florets
- 4 oz shiitake mushrooms, sliced
- 1 cup matchstick carrots (or shredded carrot)
- 1 cup cabbage, chopped into small strips
- 1 tablespoon vegetable oil

Sauce:

- 1/4 cup low sodium soy sauce
- 1/4 cup hoisin sauce
- 1 teaspoon minced garlic
- 1 teaspoon ginger, finely minced
- 3 tablespoons sriracha (more or less, depending on spice preference)
- 2 teaspoons sesame seed oil
- 2 tablespoons water

Optional garnishes:
- Chopped green onion
- Sesame seeds
- Bean sprouts or micro greens

1. In a bowl, mix together all of the sauce ingredients and set aside.

2. In a wok or large pan, heat the vegetable oil over medium-high heat. Once the oil is hot, add in the broccoli, mushrooms, carrots and cabbage and cook for about 3-4 minutes, then add in about 1/3 of the sauce and continue cooking for another 3-4 minutes.

3. Add in the udon noodles and the rest of the sauce and continue cooking for another 5 minutes. Lower the heat and add a few tablespoons of water to make it more saucy if it is a bit too thick. Top with garnishes of your choice and serve immediately.

Sesame Chili Oil Szechuan Noodles

(Vegetarian; Vegan if honey is substituted with agave)

Recipe makes 4-6 servings

- 1/2 red onion, chopped into strips
- 4 oz. shiitake mushrooms, sliced
- 4-6 baby bok choy or green cabbage, chopped
- 4 green onions, chopped
- 1 inch fresh ginger, grated
- 2 tablespoons sesame seeds
- 8 oz. wide egg noodles
- 2 tablespoons minced garlic
- 1/3 cup low-sodium soy sauce
- 1/4 cup rice vinegar
- 2 tablespoons chili oil
- 2 tablespoons honey or agave
- 2 tablespoons sesame seed oil
- 2 tablespoons olive or peanut oil
- 2 tablespoons corn starch

1. To make the sauce, combine the soy sauce, rice vinegar, honey/agave, sesame seed oil, chili oil and 1/3 cup water in a bowl and mix well.

2. In a separate bowl, whisk together 2 tablespoons of corn starch and 2 tablespoons of water. Stir until smooth, pour in with the sauce and mix well. Set aside.

3. Boil the noodles according to package directions.

4. While the noodles boil, heat the olive or peanut oil in a wok or pot over medium high heat. Add the ginger, garlic and sesame seeds and sauté for about 3 minutes or until fragrant. Next add the red and green onions and continue cooking for another 3-5 minutes. Add in the shiitake mushrooms and the baby bok choy and sauce for 5 minutes.

5. Pour the sauce in with the vegetables, lower the heat and let simmer for about 10 minutes.

6. Add the cooked noodles in with the vegetables and sauce and stir to combine.

7. Serve hot with extra sesame seeds and chopped green onion as garnishes.

Chana Masala Paratha Rolls

(Vegan)

Recipe makes 5-6 rolls

Paratha (Indian flatbread) Can substitute roti, chapati, or even tortillas.

- 1 15 oz can chickpeas, drained and rinsed
- 1/2 cup red onion, diced
- 1/2 yellow onion, diced
- 1 serrano pepper, seeded and diced
- 2/3 cup diced tomato
- 1/2 cup chopped cilantro
- 1/2 cup canned coconut milk
- 1/2 cup water
- 1 tablespoon minced garlic
- 1 teaspoon ginger, finely chopped
- 1 teaspoon garam masala
- 1 teaspoon yellow curry powder
- 1 teaspoon ground turmeric
- 1 teaspoon chili powder
- 1 teaspoon salt
- Black pepper to taste
- 1 tablespoon olive oil

Cilantro Mint Chutney: (optional dipping sauce)

- 1 bunch cilantro
- 1 cup fresh mint leaves
- 1/2 cup plain vegan yogurt (sub plain greek yogurt for non-vegan option)
- 1 jalapeño, stem and seeds removed
- 1 inch piece of ginger, peeled

- Juice of 1 lemon or lime
- 1 garlic clove
- 1 teaspoon agave (sub 1/2 teaspoon honey for non-vegan)
- Salt and black pepper to taste

To make the cilantro mint chutney, simply add all ingredients to a blender or food processor and blend until smooth. You may need to add a little water if it's too thick and blend until desired consistency is reached.

1. Heat the oil in a saucepan over medium high heat and add the onion, cooking until soft and translucent. Add the minced garlic, ginger, and serrano pepper and sauté.

2. Add in the spices and continue to cook until fragrant, about 2 minutes, then add the chickpeas, tomatoes, coconut milk and water. Cook until the tomatoes have softened and the liquid starts to thicken.

3. Mash the chickpeas with a fork or potato masher. It doesn't need to be completely mashed, as texture is a good thing, but it should be thick and chunky. Adjust the seasonings for spice and flavor, if needed, then continue cooking until thickened.

4. Heat the chapati in a skillet until warm and lightly golden, then add the chana masala and top with cilantro and red onion. Enjoy as is or pair with cilantro mint chutney.

Spicy Tahini Pasta

(Vegan)

Recipe makes approx. 4 servings

- 16 oz. spaghetti or angel hair pasta
- 2 cups fresh spinach
- 1 cup frozen peas
- 6 oz. cremini mushrooms
- Extra virgin olive oil

Spicy Tahini Sauce:

- 1 jalapeno pepper, seeded
- 1 lemon
- 1/2 cup tahini
- 1 cup water
- 3 cloves garlic
- Salt and pepper to taste

1. Boil the pasta according to package directions.

2. While the noodles boil, prepare the spicy tahini sauce by blending all ingredients in a blender or food processor. If it comes out a bit too thick just add small amounts of water until you reach your desired consistency. Set aside.

3. In a large pot, heat 2 tablespoons of extra virgin olive oil over medium heat. Once hot, add the mushrooms and sauté for about 3-4 minutes. Next, add in the frozen peas and the spinach and continue to sauté until the spinach begins to wilt and the peas are cooked through.

4. Combine the cooked pasta with the vegetables and toss with the spicy tahini sauce.

Happy Eating !
Joyce @
Vintage Green

Brussel Sprouts Power Bowl With Apple Cider Dijon Vinaigrette V+

(Vegan)

Makes about 6 servings

- 1 lb. brussel sprouts
- 1 large sweet potato, peeled and diced
- 1 avocado, sliced
- 1 cup fresh kale (or spinach)
- 1 cup dry quinoa
- 1 tablespoon dijon mustard
- 1 tablespoon pure maple syrup (or honey for a non-vegan option)
- 1 teaspoon garlic powder
- 1 tablespoon apple cider vinegar
- 1 tablespoon tahini
- Roughly 6 tablespoon extra virgin olive oil
- Salt and pepper to taste
- Pinch of cinnamon

Non-vegan optional toppings:

- Crumbled feta or goat cheese

1. Preheat the oven to 375 degrees F.
2. Cut the ends off of the brussel sprouts then cut into halves or quarters.
3. Line a large baking sheet with foil and fill half with the chopped brussel sprouts and the other half with the sweet potato. If you don't have a baking sheet large enough to fit both, just use 2 separate baking sheets. Drizzle olive oil over the veggies and season with salt and pepper. I like to sprinkle a little bit of cinnamon only on the sweet potatoes and some garlic powder only on the brussels. Toss the veggies with your hands to coat evenly with oil and seasonings and try to keep the brussels and sweet potato separated. Bake for 30 minutes, flipping the veggies half-way through.

4. While the veggies are roasting in the oven, cook the quinoa. You can use a pot on the stovetop or a rice cooker. Pour 1 cup of dry quinoa into a pot over medium high heat with 2 cups of water and a small amount of olive oil and mix with a spoon. Place the lid on the pot to cover. When it comes to a boil, lower the heat and continue cooking. The quinoa will be done when all water is absorbed and it fluffs easily with a fork.

5. While the quinoa cooks, make the vinaigrette. Combine 1 tablespoon of olive oil, apple cider vinegar, dijon mustard, honey or syrup, and tahini. Whisk together in a small bowl. Season with salt and pepper to taste.

6. Chop the kale into small pieces, removing the stems.

7. To assemble the bowls, layer the quinoa, then kale and top with the mix of brussel sprouts and sweet potato. Top slices of avocado and drizzle the vinaigrette.

Baked Spinach & Artichoke Truffle Pesto Gnocchi

(Vegetarian)

Recipe makes approx. 4 servings

- 1 lb. cauliflower gnocchi (this is a healthier version, but potato gnocchi is fine too)
- 1 12 oz can quartered artichokes, drained
- 3 cups fresh baby spinach
- 1 small white onion, diced
- 8 oz sliced portobello mushrooms
- 1 tablespoon truffle oil
- 1 15 oz can lite coconut milk
- 1 lemon
- 2 garlic cloves
- 1 teaspoon Italian seasoning
- 1/3 cup basil pesto
- 1/2 cup shredded provolone or fontina cheese
- 1/3 cup dry white cooking wine (you can use water if you prefer not to cook with wine)
- 1/2 teaspoon red pepper flakes
- Salt and pepper to taste

1. Preheat the oven to 400 degrees F.

2. Heat olive oil in a large skillet over medium-high heat. When the oil is hot, add the onion, cooking for about 5 minutes. Add the minced garlic, sliced mushrooms, Italian seasoning and red pepper flakes. Cook until slightly golden - about another 3 minutes.

3. Add the gnocchi, spinach, white wine, 1 cup of water and season with salt and black pepper.

4. Bring to a boil, cooking for about 4-5 minutes until gnocchi is soft. Add the coconut milk, truffle oil, artichokes, pesto, and lemon juice. Cook for another 5 minutes. Remove from heat and transfer to a 9x9 baking dish.

5. Top with shredded cheese and bake uncovered for 10 minutes or until the cheese is melted and sauce is bubbling.

Lettuce Wraps With Chili Peanut Sauce V+

(Vegan)

Recipe makes approx 6 servings

- 1 red bell pepper, diced
- 2 cups shredded red cabbage
- 1 cup matchstick carrots
- 4oz cremini or shiitake mushrooms, diced
- 1 head of butter lettuce
- 12 oz plant based chicken (or you can use 1 block of extra firm tofu instead. Be sure to remove as much liquid as possible, then crumble)
- 2 tablespoons minced garlic
- 4 tablespoons extra virgin olive oil, divided

Chili Peanut Sauce:

- 5 tablespoons low sodium soy sauce
- 1/2 cup peanut butter
- 2 tablespoons water
- 2 tablespoons sesame seed oil
- 2 tablespoons rice vinegar
- 1 teaspoon grated ginger
- 1 tablespoon pure maple syrup (or honey for non-vegan option)
- 1 tablespoon chili paste (sambal)

Toppings:
- Crushed peanuts
- Cilantro
- Green onion
- Lime juice

1. Start by making the chili peanut sauce by combining all ingredients in a bowl and mix until smooth. Set aside.

2. Next, add 2 tablespoons of extra virgin olive oil in a large wok or skillet over medium heat. Once hot, add the plant based chicken and diced mushrooms and cook for about 5 minutes. Next, add the minced garlic and continue cooking for about 2 minutes. Pour about 3/4 of the chili peanut sauce in with the chicken and mushrooms and stir to coat. Lower the heat and simmer, stirring occasionally while you start to cook the veggies in a separate pan.

3. In a separate nonstick pan, heat the other 2 tablespoons of extra virgin olive oil on medium heat. Once hot, add the bell pepper, cabbage and carrots and stir fry for about 5 minutes. The veggies should still be somewhat firm and crunchy, not fully cooked and soft.

4. To assemble the lettuce wraps, spoon about 2 heaping spoonfuls of the chicken mixture onto a lettuce cup, then add a spoonful of the veggie stir fry. Drizzle some of the leftover chili peanut sauce to top and add crushed peanuts, chopped green onion and cilantro. Squeeze fresh lime juice on top and enjoy!

Cheesy Broccoli & Rice Bake

(Vegan)

Recipe makes approx. 6 servings

- 2 cups broccoli florets
- 1 cup baby carrots, chopped
- 1 15 oz can chickpeas, drained and rinsed
- 2 1/2 cups low sodium vegetable stock or broth
- 1 cup brown rice, uncooked
- 1/4 cup nutritional yeast
- 3/4 cup canned lite coconut milk
- 1 teaspoon garlic powder
- 1 teaspoon onion powder
- 1/2 teaspoon paprika
- 1/2 teaspoon turmeric
- 1/2 teaspoon black pepper

1. Preheat the oven to 400 degrees F.
2. Combine all ingredients in a 9x13 baking dish and mix well, making sure the seasonings don't clump.
3. Cover the baking dish with foil and bake for 60 minutes, or until liquid is absorbed.

For a non-vegan option, sprinkle shredded cheddar cheese on top and bake uncovered for an additional 5-10 minutes, until cheese is melted.

Thai Vegetable Green Coconut Curry

(Vegan)

Recipe makes approx 6 servings

- 1.5 cups uncooked jasmine rice
- 4 tablespoons Thai green curry paste (Thai Kitchen brand is vegan, but some curry pastes are made with shrimp or fish paste, so read the label carefully to make sure you get a vegan friendly brand if you are vegan!)
- 2 cups broccoli florets
- 1 cup chopped carrot
- 1 cup sugar snap peas
- 1 red bell pepper, sliced
- 8 oz. can bamboo shoots, drained
- 2 13 oz. cans coconut milk
- 1/2 cup water or vegetable broth
- 1 inch piece of ginger, grated
- 2 teaspoons minced garlic
- 1 teaspoon ground turmeric
- 1 teaspoon brown or coconut sugar
- Salt and black pepper to taste
- 2 tablespoons extra virgin olive oil

Optional:

- Fresh basil leaves and/or green onion (for topping)
- 1 serrano pepper, diced - (adding a spicy pepper will give you authentic Thai flavor, but only do this if you like your food really spicy!)

1. Start by cooking the rice according to package directions.

2. Meanwhile, heat the olive oil over medium heat in a large pot. When the oil is hot, add the carrots, broccoli, bell pepper and serrano pepper (optional) and sauté for about 5 minutes.

3. Next, add the ginger and garlic and continue cooking for another 2 minutes. Add in the curry paste and continue to cook for another 3 minutes while stirring constantly to ensure the curry paste fully coats the veggies and becomes fragrant.

4. Next, add the coconut milk and water or vegetable broth and stir well. Add the salt, pepper, sugar, ground turmeric and the sugar snap peas and bamboo shoots. Lower the heat and place the lid on the pot, cooking for about 15 minutes, or until veggies are soft and cooked through.

5. Serve hot with rice and garnish with fresh basil leaves and green onion.

Easy Chickpea & Veggie Rice Bake V+

(Vegan)

Recipe makes approx. 6 servings

- 1 1/2 cups low sodium vegetable broth
- 1 cup chopped baby carrots
- 5 oz chopped portobello mushrooms
- 4 ribs of celery, chopped
- 1/2 white onion, chopped
- 1 15 oz. can chickpeas, drained and rinsed
- 2 tablespoon minced garlic
- 2 tablespoon nutritional yeast
- 1 cup canned lite coconut milk
- 1 cup brown or wild rice, uncooked
- 1 teaspoon. ground turmeric
- 1/2 teaspoon. Ground cumin
- 1/2 teaspoon. red pepper flakes or cayenne pepper (optional)
- Freshly cracked black pepper to taste

1. Preheat the oven to 400 degrees F.
2. Combine all ingredients in a 9x13 baking dish and mix well, making sure the seasonings don't clump.
3. Cover the baking dish with foil and bake for 60-65 minutes, or until liquid is absorbed. *For a non-vegan option, add shredded cheddar cheese on top after baking for 60 minutes and bake uncovered for an additional 5 minutes to melt.

Turmeric Sweet Potato Bowl With Lemon Vinaigrette

(Vegetarian)

Recipe makes 4 servings

- 4 eggs, cooked to your choice
- 2 medium-large sweet potatoes, peeled and chopped
- 2 cups chopped kale (or spinach)
- 2 cloves of garlic
- 1 cup wild rice (brown rice or quinoa is also great)
- 1 teaspoon ground turmeric
- 2 teaspoon pure maple syrup (or honey for non-vegan)
- 1 tablespoon garlic powder
- 1/4 cup lemon juice
- 1/3 cup olive oil
- Chopped pistachios (almonds or walnuts are also great)

1. Preheat the oven to 400 degrees F.
2. Place sweet potatoes on a lined baking sheet and toss with olive oil, turmeric, garlic powder, salt and pepper. Bake for 25 minutes, flipping halfway through.
3. While the potatoes are roasting, cook the rice or quinoa. Pour 1 cup of rice or quinoa into a small pot on medium heat with 2 cups of water, a little bit of olive oil and cover with the lid. When the water starts to boil lower the heat and cook on low-medium heat until water is absorbed and you can fluff with a fork.
4. To make the vinaigrette, combine the olive oil, lemon juice, maple syrup, minced garlic, salt and pepper in a small bowl and mix well. Set aside.
5. Next, heat olive oil in a nonstick pan over medium heat. When the olive oil is hot, add in the kale and sauté for about 3 minutes or until vibrant green and starts to wilt slightly.
6. When the sweet potatoes are finished roasting, transfer to a large mixing bowl and mash with a fork or potato masher. You may need to add a little more salt and pepper.
7. Arrange the rice, mashed sweet potato and kale in a bowl and top with 1 egg (cooked to your choice), lemon vinaigrette and crushed nuts.

Smoky Skillet Shakshuka

(Vegetarian)

Recipe makes approx. 6 servings

- 4 large tomatoes, diced
- 1 yellow onion, diced
- 2 teaspoon minced garlic
- 6 large eggs
- 1 15 oz. can cannellini beans, drained and rinsed
- 1/2 cup water
- 2 cups fresh spinach
- 1 teaspoon oregano
- 1 teaspoon ground cumin
- 1 teaspoon ground turmeric
- 1 teaspoon chili powder
- 1 teaspoon smoked paprika
- Salt and freshly cracked black pepper to taste
- 1/2 teaspoon cayenne pepper or red pepper flakes
- Crumbled feta cheese to top

Optional:

- Toasted pita bread for dipping

1. Heat olive oil in a large skillet over medium heat then add onion and cook until soft and translucent. Add in the minced garlic and cook for 1 minute.

2. Add the diced tomatoes to the skillet and cook until tomatoes get soft and start to make a sauce. You'll want to stir often and crush the tomatoes with the spoon, then simmer to allow tomatoes to make a sauce.

3. Add in the cannellini beans, along with 1/2 cup of water and all seasonings and continue cooking until the sauce starts to thicken.

4. Fold the spinach into the tomato sauce and continue cooking for a few minutes, until wilted.

5. Keeping the heat on medium, crack the eggs into the sauce after making a small pocket for the egg to go into with your spoon. Place the lid on top and let them simmer for 5 minutes, or until the egg whites are set but the yolks are still soft.

6. Top with crumbled feta cheese and toast some pita bread for dipping!

Mediterranean Grain Bowls With Tzatziki (V+)

(Vegan)

Recipe makes 4 servings

- 1 red bell pepper, chopped into 1 inch pieces
- 1 yellow squash, sliced and halved
- 1 zucchini, sliced and halved
- 1/2 red onion, chopped into 1 inch pieces
- 1 small head of cauliflower, chopped into florets
- 1 can chickpeas, drained, rinsed and patted dry with paper towel
- 1 cup wild rice or quinoa (or you can do a half and half mix!)
- 8 oz. vegan tzatziki dip, homemade or store bought
- 1 lemon
- 1 teaspoon garlic powder
- 1 teaspoon cumin
- 1 teaspoon paprika
- 1/2 teaspoon cinnamon
- Salt and pepper to taste
- Extra virgin olive oil

1. Cook the rice or quinoa according to package directions.

2. While the rice/quinoa cooks, preheat the oven to 400 degrees F

3. Chop all of the vegetables and place on a large lined baking sheet. Add the chickpeas to the baking sheet with the vegetables then drizzle with olive oil and sprinkle the seasonings. Toss well to coat evenly and bake for 30-35 minutes, flipping at 20 minutes.

4. To assemble the bowls, add the rice/quinoa with the roasted veggies, top with about 2 spoonfuls of the tzatziki and squeeze a lemon wedge over the top.

Cheesy Enchilada Quinoa Bake

(Vegetarian)

Recipe makes approx. 6 servings

- 1 cup of quinoa, uncooked
- 1 15 oz can black beans, drained and rinsed
- 1 15 oz can whole kernel corn, drained and rinsed
- 2 10 oz cans red enchilada sauce
- 1 15 oz can fire roasted tomatoes
- 4 oz can diced green chilis
- 4 oz cream cheese
- 1 cup shredded Mexican cheese
- 1/2 cup water
- 1 teaspoon ground cumin
- 1 teaspoon garlic powder
- 1 teaspoon chili powder
- Salt and black pepper to taste
- Red chili flakes (optional for heat)

Optional toppings:

- Chopped cilantro
- Avocado
- Sour cream

1. Cook the quinoa on the stovetop or in a rice cooker according to package directions.
2. Preheat oven to 375 degrees F.
3. In a large pot combine 1 can of enchilada sauce, fire roasted tomatoes, green chilies, corn, black beans, water, cream cheese, and all seasonings. Heat on medium and stir until cream cheese is fully melted.
4. Once the quinoa is cooked, add to the pot with everything else and stir to mix.
5. Pour the contents of the pot into an 11x14 casserole dish then pour the remaining can of enchilada sauce on top and sprinkle with the shredded Mexican cheese.
6. Bake uncovered for 10 minutes or until cheese is melted and bubbling.

Sweet Potato & Black Bean Burgers V+

(Vegan)

Recipe makes 6 burgers

- 1 15 oz. can black beans, drained and rinsed
- 1 large sweet potato, peeled and diced
- 1/2 cup dry, uncooked quinoa
- 1 teaspoon ground cumin
- 1 teaspoon curry powder
- 1 teaspoon ground turmeric
- 1 teaspoon garlic powder
- 1 teaspoon onion powder
- 1 teaspoon smoked paprika
- 1 teaspoon chili powder
- 1/2 teaspoon cayenne powder
- 1 teaspoon salt
- 1 teaspoon black pepper
- 2 - 3 green onions, chopped
- 1/2 bunch cilantro, chopped
- Whole grain burger buns

Options for garnishes:

- Avocado, sliced
- Red onion
- Tomato
- Romaine or butter lettuce

For the sriracha lime cream sauce:

- 5 oz. plain dairy free yogurt
- Juice of 1/2 lime
- 1 teaspoon sriracha

1. Preheat oven to 400 degrees F.

2. Add the diced sweet potato to a lined baking sheet. Drizzle with extra virgin olive oil and season with salt and black pepper. Toss to coat evenly and bake for 30 minutes, flipping halfway through.

3. While the sweet potatoes are roasting, cook 1/2 cup of quinoa with 1 cup of water in a rice cooker or in a pot with a lid over low-medium high heat.

4. Meanwhile, mash the black beans in a large mixing bowl with a fork or potato masher. You can also use a food processor. Don't worry if there are some chunks - texture is good for these!

5. When the sweet potatoes are finished roasting, add them to the bowl with black beans and mash together. Next, add the cooked quinoa, all seasonings, green onion and cilantro to the mixture and combine well. The mixture should be thick and slightly sticky.

6. Form the burger patties using your hands and place on a baking sheet (no need to grease the sheet) about 1 inch apart. Bake for 25 minutes at 350 degrees F, flipping the burgers halfway through.

7. While the burgers are baking, make the sriracha lime cream sauce by mixing the yogurt, lime juice and sriracha together in a small bowl.

8. Assemble the burgers with the toppings of your choice and the sriracha lime cream sauce and enjoy!

Stuffed Acorn Squash

(Vegetarian; Vegan if cheese is omitted)

Recipe makes 2-4 servings

- 1 whole acorn squash
- 1 cup wild rice (sub brown rice or quinoa)
- 1 15 oz can chickpeas, drained and rinsed
- 1 15 oz can black beans, drained and rinsed
- 1/2 white or red onion, chopped
- 1/4 cup chopped cilantro
- 3 green onions, chopped
- 1 tablespoon minced garlic
- 1 teaspoon cumin
- 1 teaspoon paprika
- 1/2 teaspoon turmeric
- Pinch of cinnamon
- 1/2 teaspoon cayenne pepper
- Salt and pepper to taste
- Extra virgin olive oil

Optional toppings:

- Crumbled feta or goat cheese
- Pine nuts, pumpkin or sunflower seeds
- Sliced cherry tomatoes

1. Preheat the oven to 400 degrees F.

2. After draining and rinsing the chickpeas, pat them dry with a paper towel and transfer to a lined baking sheet or small casserole dish. Drizzle with olive oil and sprinkle with salt, pepper, paprika, cumin and cayenne pepper. Toss to coat evenly and set aside.

3. To cut the acorn squash in half: Hold the acorn squash horizontally on a cutting board so that the stem is on your left and the pointy end is on your right. Cut in half using a sharp knife (this may take a few good pushes down on the knife to cut through) then cut just enough of the pointy end to make a flat surface for the squash to be able to sit upright.

4. Using a spoon, scoop out the seeds and stringy pieces from the cavities of the acorn squash and discard.

5. Rub some olive oil into the acorn squash cavities and onto the edges then season with salt and pepper. Place the acorn onto a lined baking sheet cavity side down. This will help to steam the insides while roasting. Bake the chickpeas and acorn squash at the same time for 35 minutes, or until the squash is tender.

6. Meanwhile, sauté the diced onion and garlic in a nonstick pan until soft and translucent then transfer to a large mixing bowl. Add in the black beans, cilantro, green onions and all seasonings and mix well.

7. When the squash and chickpeas finish roasting, spoon the rice mixture into the cavities of the squash, then top with the roasted chickpeas and add any additional toppings of your choice. Serve warm.

Southwestern Quinoa Stuffed Peppers

(Vegetarian; Vegan if cheese is omitted)

Recipe makes 6 whole peppers

- 6 large bell peppers
- 1 cup quinoa, uncooked
- 1 15 oz. can black beans, drained and rinsed
- 1 15 oz. can diced tomatoes
- 1 15 oz. can corn, drained and rinsed
- 1 4 oz. can green chilies (mild or hot)
- 1/2 of 1 jalapeño, chopped
- 1 small white or yellow onion, diced
- 2 tablespoons minced garlic
- 1 teaspoon ground cumin
- 1 teaspoon paprika
- 1 teaspoon chili powder
- 1 teaspoon salt
- 1/2 teaspoon black pepper
- 1/2 teaspoon cayenne pepper (optional for heat)
- Shredded Mexican or Monterrey Jack cheese to top

Optional toppings: sour cream or plain greek yogurt, salsa or hot sauce, avocado, chopped cilantro.

1. Cook the quinoa on the stovetop or in a rice cooker using 2 cups of water. Quinoa should be fluffy and all water absorbed once cooked.

2. Preheat oven to 375 degrees F.

3. Sauté the onion and jalapeño over medium heat in a pot with olive oil until soft, about 5 minutes. Add in the minced garlic and cook for another 2 minutes then add the black beans, corn, green chiles, diced tomatoes and all seasonings. Once the quinoa is cooked, add to the pot with the veggies and mix well. Remove from heat.

4. Cut the bell peppers in half lengthwise and remove the seeds. Arrange in a casserole dish with the cut side facing up, and add 1-2 tablespoons of water to the bottom of the dish to prevent the peppers from sticking while baking.

5. Spoon the filling into each pepper and sprinkle the cheese on top. Bake uncovered for 30-35 minutes, until peppers are tender and cheese is melted.

Indian Butter Vegetable Curry

(Vegan)

Recipe makes approx. 6 servings

- 1 small yellow onion, diced
- 1/2 head of cauliflower, chopped into florets
- 1 russet potato, peeled and diced
- 1 cup chopped baby carrots
- 1 small serrano or jalapeño pepper, thinly sliced
- 1 cup frozen peas
- 2 tablespoons tomato paste
- 1.5 cups vegetable broth or stock
- 1.5 cups lite coconut milk
- 1 inch of ginger, grated
- 2 tablespoons minced garlic
- 1.5 tablespoons yellow curry powder
- 1 teaspoon garam masala
- 1 teaspoon chili powder
- Salt and black pepper to taste
- Extra virgin olive oil

Serve with: basmati rice or naan and top with chopped cilantro.

1. In a large pot, add the olive oil and heat over medium high heat. Once hot, add the diced onion and cook until they start to become soft and translucent. Add in the serrano pepper, ginger and minced garlic and continue cooking for another 2 minutes.

2. Next, add the carrots, potatoes, and cauliflower to the pot and cook for about 5 minutes, stirring often. Add the tomato paste and all seasonings, making sure to coat all of the veggies until the paste starts to melt and it becomes fragrant.

3. Add in the vegetable broth and coconut milk and mix well. Place the lid on the pot and lower the heat, allowing to simmer until the vegetables are cooked through and soft.

4. Add the frozen peas and cook for another few minutes, allowing them to cook through.

5. Serve with basmati rice or naan.

Curry Cauliflower & Kale Soup Ⓥ+

(Vegan)

Recipe makes approx. 6 servings

- 1 head of cauliflower, chopped into florets then pulsed into cauliflower rice
- 1 small onion, diced
- 2 cups chopped carrots
- 1 inch piece of ginger, grated
- 1 tablespoon minced garlic
- 3 cups vegetable broth
- 1 cup canned coconut milk
- 2 cups chopped kale
- Juice of 1 lemon
- 2 teaspoons curry powder
- 1 teaspoon turmeric
- 1 teaspoon cumin
- Salt and black pepper to taste
- Red pepper flakes
- 2 tablespoons extra virgin olive oil

Optional garnish:

- Chopped cilantro

1. Heat the olive oil in a pot over medium heat, then add the onion, ginger and garlic and cook until the onions are soft and translucent.
2. Next, add in the chopped carrots and cauliflower rice with the seasonings and continue cooking for about 5 minutes.
3. Pour in the vegetable broth and coconut milk and stir well to combine. Place the lid on the pot and simmer until the vegetables are cooked through, stirring every few minutes.
4. When the veggies are soft, add in the chopped kale and the lemon juice and continue simmering for another 3-5 minutes.
5. Serve hot and garnish with chopped cilantro.

Malai Kofta

(Including both vegan/non-vegan options)

Recipe makes approx 6 servings

The authentic way to make the kofta is by using potato and paneer. Paneer is a soft, non-melting Indian cottage cheese, but because paneer is usually only available in select grocery stores or online, I am using ricotta cheese for this recipe. For a vegan option you can use firm tofu instead! The traditional way to cook them is by frying, but I am going for a healthier version so I bake mine. Either way you decide to go is fine and both ways are delicious!

Kofta:

- 1 1/4 lb Russet potatoes (usually 2 medium sized potatoes), peeled and cubed
- 16 oz. ricotta cheese OR 16 oz. firm or extra firm tofu for vegan option (squeeze water from tofu)
- 1/2 cup corn starch or arrowroot starch
- 1/4 cup chopped cilantro
- Juice of 1/2 lemon
- 2 teaspoons garam masala
- 1 teaspoon yellow curry powder
- 2 teaspoons salt (if using tofu), use less salt if using ricotta cheese
- 1 teaspoon cracked black pepper
- 1 cup frozen green peas
- Extra virgin olive oil for baking

Tomato Coconut Curry:

- 1 yellow onion, finely diced
- 28-32 oz. can diced tomatoes
- 2 tablespoons minced garlic
- 1 inch piece of ginger, finely chopped
- 2 teaspoons garam masala
- 2 teaspoons yellow curry powder

- 1 teaspoon chili powder
- 1/2 teaspoon cayenne pepper, for heat
- 1 teaspoon salt and black pepper
- 15 oz can coconut milk

1. Start by filling a pot with water and bringing to a boil over medium high heat. Add the potatoes to the boiling water and cook for about 10 minutes, or until potatoes can be easily mashed with a fork.

2. While the potatoes boil, crumble the tofu into a large mixing bowl using your hands. If using ricotta cheese, just add to the bowl. When the potatoes finish cooking, add to the tofu or ricotta and mash with a fork. Add the lemon juice, garam masala, curry powder, salt, black pepper, and cornstarch and mix well. The mixture should hold together when formed into a ball and it's ok if it sticks to your hands a bit. If the mixture is too wet, add a bit more cornstarch. Add in the cilantro and frozen peas and mix well. Form into equal sized balls using your hands and set aside.

3. Preheat the oven to 425 degrees F. Line a large baking sheet with parchment paper and spray or brush with a little bit of oil. Arrange the kofta so that there is at least 1 inch between each. Brush the tops with oil and bake for 40 minutes, flipping halfway through.

4. While the kofta is in the oven, start the tomato coconut curry sauce by adding oil to a deep nonstick pan or pot and heating to medium. When the oil is hot add the onion and sauté for about 5 minutes. When the onions start to get a little golden, add in the minced garlic, ginger and the spices and continue cooking for about 3-4 more minutes. Next add the canned tomatoes and all of the juice, cover with the lid and let simmer for about 15 minutes, stirring occasionally.

5. Transfer the onion and tomato mixture to a blender and blend until smooth. Make sure you leave a vent in the lid of the blender by removing the center piece on the lid or opening up the vent lid if your blender top has one. Cover the vent with a towel before blending to prevent splatter. This is important to do when blending hot liquids to prevent cracking the blender! Once smooth, add back to the pan and add in the coconut milk. Stir to mix and leave on low heat until the kofta are ready.

6. To serve, pour the sauce into a bowl and add the kofta. Garnish with chopped cilantro and/ or naan and enjoy hot! (Only add the kofta to the sauce that you will eat per meal. Keep the kofta and sauce separate when refrigerating, and also reheat separately otherwise the kofta will become soggy.)

Bombay Wraps (V+)

(Vegan)

Recipe makes approx. 6 wraps

- 2 medium sized russet potatoes, peeled and diced
- 1 head of cauliflower, chopped into florets
- 1 15 oz can chickpeas, drained and rinsed
- Fresh baby spinach
- 3 tablespoons yellow curry powder, divided
- 1 teaspoon garam masala
- 1 tablespoon cumin
- 1 tablespoon smoked paprika
- 1 teaspoon ground turmeric
- 1 teaspoon garlic powder
- 2 tablespoons vegan butter
- 1 teaspoon salt
- 1 teaspoon black pepper
- Whole wheat tortillas

Cilantro Mint Chutney:

- 1 bunch cilantro
- 1 cup fresh mint leaves
- 1/2 cup plain vegan yogurt (sub plain greek yogurt for non-vegan option)
- 1 jalapeño, stem and seeds removed
- 1 inch piece of ginger, peeled
- Juice of 1 lemon or lime
- 1 garlic clove
- 1 teaspoon agave (sub 1/2 teaspoon honey for non-vegan)
- Salt and black pepper to taste

To make the mint chutney, simply add all ingredients to a blender or food processor and blend until smooth. You may need to add a little water if it's too thick and blend until desired consistency is reached. This sauce is so delicious and it takes no more than 2 minutes to make! I'm telling you, you don't want to skip the sauce here! It really completes the dish.

1. Preheat the oven to 400 degrees F and fill a medium to large sized pot with enough water to boil the potatoes. Place the pot of water over medium-high heat and boil the potatoes.

2. Meanwhile, add the cauliflower to a large, lined baking sheet.

3. Drain and rinse the chickpeas well, then pat dry with paper towel and add to the baking sheet with the cauliflower. Drizzle the cauliflower and chickpeas with olive oil and season with garam masala, cumin, paprika, salt, pepper, and 1 tablespoon of the yellow curry powder. Roast for 30 minutes, tossing halfway through.

4. Remove the potatoes from water when fully cooked and transfer to a large mixing bowl. Mash the potatoes well and add in the butter, garlic powder, turmeric and 2 tablespoons of the yellow curry powder and mix well.

5. To assemble the wraps, spread the curry mashed potatoes on the tortilla, then lay a bed of fresh spinach on top. Add the roasted chickpeas and cauliflower then top with the cilantro mint chutney.

Curry Vegetable Pot Pies

(Vegan)

Recipe makes 4 individual pies

- 1 box frozen vegan puff pastry (2 sheets)
- 4 individual pie tins, 4x4
- 1 15 oz can lite coconut milk
- 1 12 oz bag mixed frozen peas & carrots
- 1 medium potato, peeled and diced
- 1 small - medium white onion, diced
- 2 garlic cloves
- 2 teaspoons curry powder
- 1/2 teaspoon ground turmeric
- 1 teaspoon ground cumin
- 1/2 teaspoon cayenne pepper or red pepper flakes
- 1/2 teaspoon salt
- 1/2 teaspoon black pepper
- Vegan butter (optional)

1. Remove the frozen puff pastry from the freezer to thaw.

2. In a large non-stick pan on medium-high heat, add olive oil and sauté the diced onion until translucent. Next add the minced garlic and potatoes and continue cooking for about 5 minutes. Add the curry powder, cumin, turmeric and cayenne pepper and mix until the veggies are covered and fragrant.

3. Add the coconut milk and mix well. Lower the heat and simmer until the coconut milk starts to thicken - roughly 10 minutes. Add in the frozen peas and carrots, salt and pepper and mix well. Place a lid on the pan and continue to simmer for another 10 minutes, or until veggies are soft. Set aside and let the mixture cool a bit while preparing the pies.

4. Preheat the oven to 350 degrees F.

5. To make the pies, place the puff pastry sheets on parchment paper and roll out with a rolling pin to make the dough stretch a little. On one sheet of dough you will need to use the pie tins to measure 4 circles that are the same size as the top of the tin (used as the top of the pie). On the other sheet you will need to measure 4 circles that are about 1/2 inch larger around the top

of the pie tins to use for the base of the pie. Cut the dough with a knife or pizza cutter. Grease the pie tins well with a non-stick spray and then line the bottoms of the tins with the larger pieces of dough, pressing them into the tin.

6. Spoon in equal amounts of the veggie mixture into the pies until the tins are filled, then place the top piece of the pie onto the tin and press the edges down with a fork.

7. Cut slits into the tops of each pie to allow steam to be released while baking and you can brush the tops with melted vegan butter or dairy-free milk. For a non vegan option, you can use regular butter or an egg wash. Bake for 25 minutes or until the tops are golden.

Roasted Chili Honey Brussel Sprouts With Goat Cheese

(Vegetarian)

- 1 lb. brussel sprouts
- 1/2 teaspoon garlic powder
- 2 tablespoons olive oil
- 3 tablespoons pure maple syrup or honey
- 2 tablespoons chili paste
- 4 oz crumbled goat cheese
- Salt and black pepper to taste

1. Preheat oven to 400 degrees F.
2. Cut the brussel sprouts in halves or quarters, then place on a lined baking sheet.
3. Drizzle the brussels with olive oil, salt, pepper and garlic powder then toss with your hands to evenly coat.
4. Bake for 20 minutes, tossing halfway through.
5. In a small bowl, combine the chili paste and honey then drizzle over the roasted brussel sprouts. Toss to coat and top with crumbled goat cheese.